IOANA PREDESCU

The "Nice to meet you" interview

About interviews,
for candidates and interviewers

ISBN – 13: 978-1492964414

CONTENTS

I AM THE IDEAL CANDIDATE!

„I will not be a common man. I will stir the smooth sands of monotony"

Peter O'Toole

How many times have you woke up in the morning filled with enthusiasm because you were preparing for an interview that was supposed to get you your dream job? You left home confident, you arrived with great punctuality, you have smiled and showed diligence as you have patiently answered all questions and then, after the well-known „Thank you for your time. We will get back to you shortly", you left already anxious to receive the telephone announcing you about being selected.

For the next few days you thought about your new colleagues, your new salary, you made plans......

And the days went by and the telephone is yet to ring. You started to think about the reasons of delay. But when the reasons dried out, the truth revealed itself with disappointment: you have not been selected.

Of course, you wanted to know why, but when you receive an answer, it is probably "We selected another candidate with more relevant experience in the job-specific areas".

What the employer wants to say is "We have selected a candidate whose abilities and experience have been *presented to us in such manner* that we are convinced the he/she is the best fit."

But what if you could deliberately influence the result of an interview? How exactly? Start with yourself:

1. Be aware of your value
2. Be aware of your personality
3. Be very sure about what you want (in your career)
4. Make your behaviour consistent with your wishes
5. Make a selection
6. Create a stunning Resume
7. Take as many interviews as possible
8. Do your homework
9. Find out more during the interview

10. Generate the feed-back after the interview

Let's discuss about each of the 10 points.

1. Be aware of your value

Your value is what makes the difference between you and the other candidates. Of course, you don't know the other candidates, but be sure there's a ranking in place. The employer makes a ranking and decides according to it.

Even though "the truth has the habit of revealing itself" a little help now and then is a good idea. The first step is for one person to be aware of one's professional qualities and flaws.

You have studied, and prepared for years for a specific professional area, you have attended university classes or technical schools where you have acquired knowledge and abilities. You must "display" this knowledge and these abilities.

Of course, value is constantly growing. Ambitious people, who aim to succeed in life, are continuously studying and improving.

But the value you give yourself is the starting point of the value others assign to you. If you do not consider yourself a professional, then you are probably not, but then you will have to revise your professional aspirations.

So start by being fully aware of your own value. Only when you know your place in the profession group, you will understand better many aspects of your present and future professional life.

Let's take an exercise: close your eyes and think about what it is you do best. Then imagine yourself doing that. Picture the result of the work you value the most. Now look in the mirror and see the change on your face.

When your mind focuses on success, your entire body feels the benefits of that success. You are more optimistic, more flexible, more open and more pleasant and you will continue to have success after success.

Maintain and perfect these professional treats and you will experience a sequence of "successes". Spend 30 minutes of your day studying and you will come to experience spectacular beneficial effects. The people around you will see it too and will come closer.

*****

Now let's think – objectively – about your flaws. Take a notebook, which you will call "my career". Write on the first page, big and beautiful, what is it that you want to obtain in your professional life. What is your ultimate goal? What is it you dream to be?

Now go to the next page and write the skills and the knowledge which you believe necessary to achieve and to maintain that stage. Keep the list open – as time passes, you will add other skills and knowledge which you will find useful.

Now on another page, make a list with the skills and knowledge which you already possess. Be honest with yourself and write down as objectively as possible what you have acquired so far.

Compare the two lists and see what is missing or what is not enough and needs more work. Then, for each of those, write down which is the part of your career that will benefit the most from it. Then, assess the effort you need to invest in improving that particular skill or knowledge area and which is higher: the benefit or the effort.

Now, all you have to do, is act on it. Being aware of your flaws, you can now stop referring to them as flaws, and work towards their elimination. Study, experiment, exercise, improve yourself continuously.

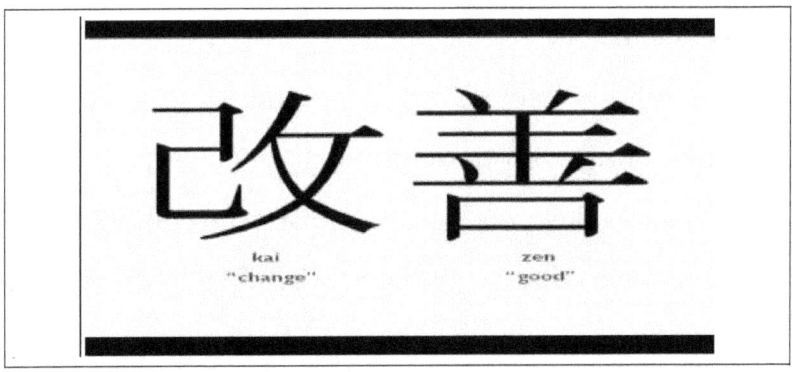

Every successful person has flaws or areas they do not master, but these people are doing something different then the rest of us: they continuously improve themselves. To identify your weak points is a valuable exercise of objectivity and self-scrutiny, but this is not enough to make you successful in the future. For this, the next step is essential: transform your weaknesses in opportunities. If this doesn't work out, at least transform them in neutral areas of your professional self.

Nobody is perfect. During your career, you are not competing with perfect people, but with "normal" people, just like you. The level of your professional improvement will decide the professional status which you will obtain. It is only your decision where to stop, based on the value you give yourself and based on what you wrote on the first page of the notebook.

2. Be aware of your personality

Your personality is the aggregate from all your moral and intellectual traits, which make you the unique person you are. That is because before you are an engineer, physician, economist, mechanic, mason, etc. you are a person. Each of is a mix of features which create our character.

Ideally, you knew yourself very well before you chose your profession.

Why do you think that the professional recruiting agencies ask the candidates to take some tests in order to determine their "personality profile"? Because some profiles are compatible with some professions and specific cultures, while others are not.

For example, a strong choleric[1] can be a great explorer but will make a frustrated accountant, drowned under a pile of papers, unless he has a melancholic side as well. On the other hand, a melancholic can be a great statistician and a very fine analyst, but is bound to fail as television moderator, for example, due to his view on human relations.

My point is: try to see if you fit the profile of the job you desire. Then, develop those features of your personality which can most likely bring you the success in that profession, exactly in the same manner you address your skills and your knowledge.

After you have chosen your profession, you must make a conscious choice about the environment in which you would like to work. Although many of us will not admit it, the environment and the circumstances will have an impact on our performance. So, try to find out what kind of

---

[1] Florence Littauer, "Personality Plus – Understanding others by understanding yourself", Fleming H. Revell

behavioural values are encouraged in the company you target, and see if you can relate to them.

I am surprised to acknowledge that in Romania such information is very difficult to obtain in a manner more reliable than a rumour. The companies are reluctant to divulge information such as rules of conduct, and the candidates are only aware of the information released as image campaign. Under these circumstances, many candidates are facing surprises in their first days as a new employee, and if they are not willing to accept the compromise, then the time spent during candidate selection phases gets wasted away.

The actual negotiation, for employment contracts, does not really take place, companies being pretty inflexible with the offered packages. So, what you can do is to find out as much as you can about the companies who advertise vacancies and to make your own selection, so you make sure the time you spend on interviews is well invested.

There are numerous internet sites who can provide personality tests and a series of book where the qualities and flaws of each profile are explained. You will better understand your aspirations and you will know what you need to do to gain professional growth.

When you come to an interview fully aware of your value and your personality, you will appear as a well-balanced person, who feels good in their own shoes. You will avoid looking like a teenager who tries hard to impress the parents.

3. Be very sure about what you want (in your career)

Now that you know well both your professional value and your personality, you must identify exactly what are your career expectations, how important is it for you and how much effort are you willing to invest in order to make it happen. This will help you stay focused and avoid wasting your energy with useless activities. Some people want to come to the top of the pyramid, whereas others do not see this as a priority. Each hierarchical step brings more responsibility along with the advantages which are obvious to everybody.

Make a parallel with the school grades. Let's assume that during middle school you had a constant performance. Then your pace needed to be increased to be good enough to be accepted in the high-school you chose. And you made it. But hey! In the first year of high-school you realized that the increased pace was now needed to maintain your level. Then, in the last year of high-school, your effort doubled again to be accepted in a college of choice. And that's it? Of course not! The doubled effort became the college routine and was increased again for the graduation exam.

So every next level brought in more responsibility and an increased pace. You must be aware of this before you decide what is it that you want from your career and you must be ready to face all the challenges. Nothing in life comes for free and you must be ready to pay the price for it.

On the other hand, nothing can make a worst impression to a potential employer than a candidate who had no idea what he wants and is willing to accept any position under any circumstances. In some companies, you may even be offered a number of positions in various fields and if you fall in the trap, your label will be "undecided", which is not exactly to your advantage.

But if you are coming to an interview sure about what you want, aware of what that position means, you will for sure be "labelled" as professional. Of course, provided that points 1 & 2 are met, so that your expectations are realistic.

In this context the other extreme is a candidate with an arrogant attitude who reveals his salary expectations in the first 5 minutes, of course in the context of his sky-high "value" and who has a very exaggerated self-image. It's very likely that this candidate makes a very bad impression as well in most cases.

4. Make your behaviour consistent with your wishes

Let's assume that two people make you a business proposition for a "very profitable idea". One of them is a very thorough person, who provides you with a number of graphic analysis, studies and financial compilations to prove the idea is viable, but is 20 minutes late for your meeting, looks like has just returned from a fishing trip and keeps reminding you that he needs this project to correct his problematic financial situation. The other person hands you a one-pager to present the idea, your part of the investment and the expected profit, gives you a business card and apologizes that he needs to be brief as he has other meetings pending. He assures you that once you gave it more thought you will come to the conclusion that this is a good opportunity and asks that you give an answer within three days so that he can look elsewhere for financial resources in case you chose not to be involved.

Which of the two has convinced you? Who looks more trustworthy?

Why is it that the first person lacks advantage in this discussion? Because he did not act like a business man. Maybe the idea was brilliant, maybe the research was impeccable, but he did not look like a business man. Whereas the second person, while you have no information about his experience, even though he did not present any research to sustain the project, LOOKS like a busy and trustworthy person, isn't it?

Some of you will now think that this ratiocination is not very logical. But people are not very logical beings. Or else the "first impression" would not be so powerful and would not receive so much importance. It is elegant and noble to not judge the people by appearances, but don't we do this 100 times a day? Sure, "the system" can be changed if you disagree, but in order to be able to do this, you must find yourself in such a powerful position and to get there, you need to play by the rules, at least partly.

So, if you come to an interview for a financial manager position, be sure to look, think and speak like a financial manager. If you come for a secretarial position wearing shorts, you would probably be unsuccessful even if you speak four foreign languages and can type at impressive speed. The same as if you arrive at a contest for country music wearing Armani, the jury would probably think you are lost (and they would be right).

The theory says that the form _without_ the substance[2] is useless, it doesn't say that the form doesn't matter. Per contra, it matters a great deal and it supports the content (the substance).

---

[2]Maiorescu, Titu, "*Against nowadays direction in Romanian culture*", 1978, p 153

5. Make a selection

Before you decide to apply for a job vacancy, make a selection of available positions which may be of interest to you. Consider all you know about yourself and about the companies recruiting.

Probably some of you are thinking now: "I am desperate for a job and she would consider making a selection!". It depends what you want: just any job, or a phase of career. If all you want is another job, then you can simply "go out there" and for sure you will find a job.

But if you intend to build a career, then your steps must be calculated. Parenthetically, when building a career it is recommended that the positions are back-to-back. Do not resign unless you have an offer in your hands, unless you are facing an extreme situations. This comes also with better freedom of choice. Make an analysis of your career so far and follow the steps 1 – 4 above. Then decide where you are today in the pyramid and identify what you need to continue your climb. Then try to understand which of the positions available are fit for your next steps, and apply only to those.

Do not be afraid of challenges. Even if a job comes with some tasks in areas where you are still learning, if you can improve yourself fast, go for it. Brave people are successful. They are not afraid of challenges and are confident in themselves, in their own abilities. If in doubt, then go back to section 1.

If you are building a career, get used to objective analysis before acting. Create for yourself the mentality of a successful person and make your own selection of employers before you send out your application. Create a hierarchy of the vacancies according to your professional and personal priorities. It is not very complicated and it will not take too long.

Then go for the vacancies, top down in your ranking. By applying to more positions fit for your ambitions, you will have more chances of obtaining such a position.

For sure, this becomes more difficult when so many vacancies are published without the name of the employer and while there are so many recruiting agencies using the "our client" expression. But in many cases it can be done and it will work to your advantage.

6. Create a stunning Resume

As common practice, a *recruiting officer* will give maximum 1 minute to each Resume, for the initial selection also known as *screening*. **1 minute!** This is how long you have to gain the attention of your employer, through your Resume. The main purpose of any Resume sent is to "produce" an interview. This is why it was created and why you sent it out. Have this in mind when you write it! If you feel you cannot be objective enough, ask your relatives and friends for help: ask them to pretend to be an employer and to tell you whether reading your Resume, they would want to invite you for an interview. It is time to be your most fastidious critique and rework it until you are absolutely sure that your Resume will generate interest in the recruiter's mind.

There are numerous books and whitepapers about how a Resume must look like and what exactly must it contain. There is even an "European Template" adopted as well in Romania back in 2008. But, as in all other aspects of our lives, balance is the key. The framing, the wording and the content of your Resume must be consistent with each other and with the targeted vacancy. The Resume of a Painter will look very differently than the one of an engineer.

One of the shortcomings of the modern data bases is exactly the standardization of the Resume styles. Some of them provide even linguistic innovations which make Mr. Pruteanu[3] very right speaking about the controversial bill he generated. Reading a Resume I see something similar to "I have *antrenated* people" which would come from the Romanian word for *trained.* So, during the interview I have asked this person what did she mean and she told me that the internet site where she applied, provided

---

[3] http://en.wikipedia.org/wiki/George_Pruteanu

limited options in some fields of the Resume, and this was one of those options. She apologized, being aware of torturing the mother-tongue and I have come to the appropriate conclusion. This is one of the reasons why I suggest you take each opportunity to send your "original design Resume" and make it your upper hand.

The first golden rule when creating your stunning Resume is that you do not have only one, but one for each vacancy you target. Each time you apply, go through your Resume again and make it emphasize those particular skills which are required for this particular vacancy. Remember that the package strengthens the content.

Another golden rule when creating a stunning Resume is, consistent with many other life areas, the respect you show to others. Think about the person reading your Resume, about how busy they are and do not assault them with useless information. Please choose quality over quantity. Be concise and stay focused. It is not necessary to write the story of your like, or to list each professional experience and each 2 hours workshop you have attended. Present only the most relevant information set. You can keep track (in the career notebook – see page 10) in all details, all professional projects, all education events etc. from which you then chose the ones most relevant for a certain job description.

It is also important here to remind you that the Resume is not the place to emphasize why you have decided to apply (for that we have the Motivation Letter), but it is the place to emphasize those reasons which make you the ideal candidate (without actually using this collocation). Of course, the other extreme is also a bad idea: concise, in this context is different than shallow or laconic. Just listing your school name and "previous jobs" is uninteresting and represents an unfortunate choice.

The third golden rule is keeping it real. I remember how I interviewed a candidate for a position of logistic assistant, who imagined the title would be logistic manager (!) who had provided us with an impressive list of clients served in his current position (which he was ready to leave behind). My employer back then had daily deliveries of at least 8 trucks – and the peak times doubled it and when I asked the candidate how many trucks his team had to prepare in one day he answered proudly "three". His Resume was well built and had achieved the purpose – to be invited for an interview, but the negative impression was so strong that if I would have seen this Resume again in the next two years, I would have rejected it instantly.

So, do not overbid! Present the reality, in the most favourable way for you, but stick with the reality no matter how tempting it gets the other option.

I stop here with the recommendations for Resume creation, but take your time and read the dedicated publications available on the market.

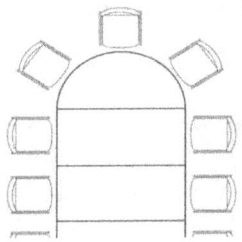

7. Take as many interviews as possible

As grandma taught us, „practice makes perfect". Even if we would like to behave very natural during an interview, this is not as easy as it sounds.

When you are attending „the interview of your life", you are nervous, you are trying to think positive and (preferably) you speak about all the important points you have planned to emphasize during the meeting.

Once you get there, any small detail which does not fit your mental plan, can drive you out of the fragile balance you have found. The employer will anyway know if you're nervous or if you lack personal confidence. For some employers this is important and for some others it is not. The issue here, is that you don't know exactly how important it is for **this one.**

My open advice is to take as many meetings and interviews as possible. Doing this, will enable you to reach some very important key aspects:

- you will become familiar with various areas in the city and you will be able to better assess the time needed to travel, and be punctual;

- you will become acquainted to various discussion „environments" from large meeting rooms to tiny offices; some warm, some cold; some quiet, some noisy etc.

- You will meet various interviewer personalities – there are several interviewing techniques – you may want to look it up;

- comparing different discussions/ interviews you can come across many aspects useful for your future: what you could have said more, or better, where your plan didn't work a.s.o.

As for the recruiting companies, it is a very good idea to meet them and to discuss with them whenever you have the chance. For example, when I am contacted for a position which I find not interesting, my answer is always „it is a pleasure to meet you and I gladly accept, but this position is not interesting for me". In this way I show respect for their time and mine and, in most of the situations, the recruiter chooses to meet me.

After a while, when you find yourself going to an interview for a very important position, you will be able to paint the picture you planned for yourself.

Hang-in-there

8. Do your homework

This point is a direct consequence of the step number 5 – the selection, but it deserves special attention.

Many times the employers are asking you „what do you know about us?" and many times your answers starts with „nothing much..." or with „just that....". Any recruiter thinks now about the enthusiasm you have shown in the cover letter about the „career opportunity" and your „desire to become part of such a professional team" and how you „adhere to the corporate values" etc. which loses the majority of the meaning if you actually know „little" or „nothing much" about the company, its business environment, its products etc.

Nowadays, at least some information are available to the public. If you apply for a „mysterious" job, be very careful about how you phrase your cover letter, to avoid embarrassing situations like the ones I have described above.

Any employer appreciates a candidate which has spent some time to learn some things about the targeted company. Such behavior shows a professional approach, an organized and serious person, which is very likely to be transformed into selection criteria.

On top of that, before the interview, organize your thoughts around the tasks you believe belong to that specific position. Write them down, so that you can answer the questions more fluently. This will help you emphasize your skills and abilities for this specific job.

Think about what kind of „professional tests" you may be asked to take, and review the possible content. You will make sure that you don't miss anything.

All of this will help you answer the questions promptly and down to the point, avoiding the areas where you feel insecure and „skipping" your „weaknesses". I recommend all candidates to avoid a direct answer to the question „what are your weaknesses". Why? Because the purpose of your being present in that meeting is to present the arguments which make you the best candidate for the job. Often enough this question is used as a trap and even when the candidate is honest, the interviewer will think that an acknowledged weakness is probably more serious than the candidate is willing to admit.

So: gather information and put them in order, to use them later to your advantage. You will need this information anyway, to make the selection described at section 5; so use them to your benefit during the interview.

9. Find out more during the interview

Do not settle for what they tell you. Companies also sell their image on the market. Each employer will tell you first those strong reasons that will make you really, really want the job.

Try to read between the lines to make your own opinion the way they work, the internal culture, the true values of the organization (and not necessarily the ones advertised). This type of information, coming on top of what you already know, are valuable and complete the picture of the employer.

Just like you, the interviewer will want the control over the meeting and, if their skills allow it, will play their role very well, carefully observing each of your reactions – after all, you are there to be assessed. Here is something that many candidates do not dare to think: **you are the assessor of that company**. The meeting is a power game where each person tries to influence the other's reactions, to understand them better – or at least, this is what it is meant to be (but not a war).

When you think about your job, how do you imagine it? Write on your notebook: your desk / office, colleagues, tasks, environment, achievements, projects, challenges etc. (we assume that your expectations are realistic even if they are bold). Afterwards think about what matters most to you – a question which is often asked in the employment questionnaires.

Having this in mind very clearly, it will be a lot easier to „decrypt" the important messages and to make up your mind (or at least to know what to expect). You should keep in mind that aiming for your reactions, the interviewer will play roles, so you are not in a position to create an objective opinion about this particular person; and sometimes not even about the job itself, before the firm offer.

There are, also, very few cases when the actual offer for employment does not depend on the candidate. In other words, there are very few companies so inflexible that they look for the person to fit the job as described. The majority of the employers are looking for a „chief accountant" or „a salesman" or „a secretary" and not for „a chief accountant which will increase budget efficiency by 3%, will wish for the corner office, would have more than 5 years' experience and would worth at least...... money in wages"; not looking for „a salesman who will triple the volume on the area X and will work heavily on optimizing the portfolio"; not for „a secretary who will rearrange the reception area on ergonomic principles, will calm down the irritated visitors , will best apply archiving principles...". Of course, it is possible that once you were hired to receive tasks like „please finish the P&L report by the 10th", or „your target is to double the volume" or „please be nice when answering the telephone", that is absolutely normal. But what I am trying to emphasize is that even if it looks unprofessional, the job design may also depend on you; and this is why you need to be prepared to bring your strengths on the table. Be prepared to push those buttons that will trigger a very good employment offer.

At some point, you can try to take control of the discussion – elegantly but firmly, asking questions which will generate answers containing the information you need. It goes without saying, this does not mean to interrupt your interlocutor or to be rude in any way. You can either wait your turn to ask the questions, or you can say from the beginning of the interview that you would like to have some time for your questions, before the interview is over.

You don't have to take any job, under any circumstances. The employer will have a good impression on a determined person, who knows what they're looking for and who is even ready to let go of an unsuitable offer.

The key learning point of this chapter: do not leave things to chance! You can act and guide them in the right direction.

10. Generate the feed-back after the interview

Has it ever happened to you to wait forever for the promised call after the interview? Have you asked yourself a million questions: „why are they not calling?", „why did they not choose me?", „have they reached a decision already?" etc. I wonder what exactly has been stopping you from making a call and asking a question about the status of the project? Have you considered that delaying the call may be a test?

For some jobs, we want people with strong determination, initiative, action etc. So, from this perspective, a person who is accepting a telephone call which never comes, will not be the ideal candidate.

It is very likely that your call will be unable to change a decision if already taken, but equally possible, it will help you foster the self-image, attitude and mentality, eventually leading you to future success.

The success is rather a journey than a destination. Everything you study, all skills that you use on your way to success, they will help you **maintain** it. You will never come to the moment when you say „There! Now I am successful; from now on, I don't have to do anything". Always remember this: the pyramid is narrower to the top and even if there are many who want to be on top, fewer get there and even fewer manage to stay there!

Therefore, you will have to decide what exactly means to you to be successful, and to be ready to pay the price for it. You will, then, have to be aware that you must never stop.

The success is an **effect** of a group of healthy habits you have consistently applied. I will close this topic with a quote of the honorable Winston Churchill: „success consists of going from failure to failure without loss of enthusiasm".

LOOKING FOR THE BEST MATCH!

„Luck is nothing but a greater attention to detail"[1]

Sir W. Churchill

---

[1] I remember reading this quote many years ago. I served me well through my teen years and all my career. Lately I was unable to trace it for documentation and proof that it actually belongs to Sir Churchill, but nevertheless, I find it tremendously useful.

What exactly „best match" for a job means? The answer to this question is of a very subjective nature, but few general traits became widely accepted: serious, punctual, hardworking, loyal etc. As you may notice, none of these refers to the professional competency, although in its absence, the person will be unable to successfully perform their daily tasks. But what does this mean, again? This reveals once more the predominantly emotional nature of all our decisions. It is not enough to be the best in our field. Among the selection criteria, often we find „ability to make relationships" or „team compatibility", which is also perfectly reasonable.

But when you are drafting a job ad to attract candidates or when you prepare (!) for a series of interviews, what could you do to make the candidates' perception about the job to be as close as possible to reality and thus, to what would mean „the best match".

The truth is that there is no universal approach to a successful recruiting process. This is also one of the reasons why sometimes it takes too long to recruit / select the right candidate whereas other times it goes very fast. Still, there are some general behavioural guidelines which could help you greatly increase the efficiency of this process. I will refer to them in the following pages.

You will not find here „magical" tests, success phrases, outfits that never fail or decision algorithms that will guarantee your success. But you will definitely find useful advice about aspects very known to you I am sure, but maybe you never actually paid enough attention to.

Very important – applying only what is written in this book and ignoring any procedural and scientific aspects, is totally wrong. This book comes on top of what you have studied, built and applied for years. This book is not a „success recipe", but rather the fine tuning.

Once you have adhered to these principles and you have started to apply them, you must do this consistently in all the fields related to the company image and the advertisement of it. Recruitment and selection, if used intelligently, can be included in the PR strategy of any company and certainly, intentionally or not, they affect (positively or negatively) the image of your company . It is therefore of utmost importance that the messages sent out through these two processes to be consistent with the other messages distributed via other PR communication channels.

The most frequent mistake made in the recruiting/selection process is „overestimation". The description of the job is inflated hoping to attract very qualified candidates. But do you really need security guards with a university degree (an intentional exaggeration)?

Another important error is ignoring the preliminary selection, which leads to a large number of useless interviews, creating fatigue and stress which, may affect the decision in the end. Or, the opposite –

the preliminary selection is too drastic and from 100 CVs, only 2 or 3 make it to the interview, creating frustrations in-house, related to perceived difficulties in choosing personnel of an appropriate profile.

Some employers overuse candidate testing during the selection process and some others do not use it at all. There is a balance point between the complexity of the job and the level of psychometric / professional testing involved.

Then, after the selection is over, the majority of the employers are tempted to contact only the selected candidates, ignoring the others. I wonder why is that? Do the persons called for interview not deserve the courtesy of being communicated the decision?

Do those candidates which were not selected, not deserve to understand the reasons behind your decision? Organizations with traditions communicate through written letters to all candidates the decisions after each step of the process. It is a matter of professionalism and respect towards people who showed interest in your company and your vacancies.

Going back to our primary focus, the interview: How should such a selection interview unfold? Of course you master the techniques of asking questions and you are able to take the discussion wherever needed. But are the questions the only ones that matter? What exactly do we prefer: a cold and strict interview or a rather casual and informal discussion? How far may the power game go and how justified are certain questions? Which are the traps set up by the so called „standard" questioning techniques? Here is what we will discuss further:

1. Appearance matters
2. Show respect for the candidates
3. Prepare for the interview
4. Avoid clichés
5. Be honest and prudent when making promises
6. Use the discussion time efficiently
7. Be aware of the company culture

8. Avoid monologues

9. Take notes

10. Smile

Just as we did in the first part, we will now discuss the above one by one.

1. APPEARANCE MATTERS

Maybe you are familiar with the „theory of substanceless forms"[2] which brought revolution to the Romanian society in the late 19th– early 20th century. But what to do about „formless substance"?

Marketing is frequently using the term „notoriety" and claims that it is something built in time, from all departments of the company and that it is strongly connected to the branding / image strategy of the company. Still, few individuals are interested to read about it, unless they are directly involved.

The public perception about any company („the image") depends on each detail considered unimportant. The image is not only the result of a conscious and systematic approach, but especially the one created unconsciously. Everything adds to the overall image, from the office space design to the

---

[2]Maiorescu, Titu, *"Against nowadays direction in Romanian culture"*, 1978, p 153

outfits of your employees; from the internal rules and regulations to each employee's behaviour outside office hours.

People generally take emotional decisions, even if they try to give them an objective tone. When someone must make a choice, they will consider the environment, the colleagues, the location, the benefits etc. So, when you start recruiting/selecting, you must know the picture you are creating through the ad, the interview room, the interviewer's look etc.

Say you are interviewing candidates for a middle management position. This particular candidate seems like the right person for the jobs, looks interested and appreciates the other aspects. Just as you were talking about the professionalism of the management team and about the wonderful career perspectives that any strong performer has in your company, few colleagues pass by the corridor speaking...."kindly" about the general manager for the latest decision. What do you think will remember the candidate: your words or the context?

The first thing you must keep in mind when preparing for a series of interviews is the picture you send out. It must fit the profile of the best match. Do not leave things to chance and do not „hope" to make a good impression, but make sure that you create the perception. From the „smell" of the room to your gestures, all must be consistent and transmit the same message. This is the safest way to add weight to your words.

I remember a selection process where I was the candidate. It was a well-known company in Bucharest, Romania and I usually accept such meetings – as mentioned in the first half of the book. So, I take the interview and I also accept a written test. In the testing day, I waited for 20 minutes in the reception until a nice young lady sees me to the testing room. We arrive to something like a hallway with coffee tables lined-up on one side, where many people were being tested for various jobs. On the floor there were piles of documents more or less filed. From time to time someone passed by, going down some stairs to the basement. I finish my test and another nice young lady came and presented herself as the interviewer. We start „searching for a meeting room" and after 15 – 20 minutes we find one and start our discussion. After another 10 minutes we are being interrupted by someone claiming the room and we start searching for another one, which we find few stores up, still bearing the marks of the previous meeting, with plastic cups, napkins and breadcrumbs on the table. At this point it was very clear to me that I will not work for this company, but like a cherry on the cake, only at the end of our conversation, the nice lady tells me that we are discussing about a temporary position but assures me that „usually such limited contracts are being prolonged".

From my perspective this company entered on a top position on my black list, for unlimited time. I accept that not everyone is being bothered by such behaviour and that some others will find their career spring-board in that environment. From my point of view this company does not have respect as an organizational value. The responsibility is also mine that I had not thoroughly checked facts about the company prior to the interview, but my point is that the employer must be consistent in all types of messages from verbal to non-verbal.

Think hard about what kind of picture you would like to shape in the minds of your candidates and check if you can sustain it by non-verbal hints as well. If not, reconsider.

2. Show respect for the candidates

I can see your lifted eyebrow. What do you mean? They applied because they need a job, right? Right, of course, but do you really have to use that to be impolite? Of course not.

Any candidate, for any job, no matter how low in the hierarchy is a person – a human being. You too, before being a „manager" or a „recruiter" or a „warehouse manager" a.s.o, you are a person and you have a moral obligation to behave properly to anyone. Not only the candidate is in need (for a job); your company is also in need (of a new employee). There is a mutual need in discussion.

Show respect for the candidate's age, even if they are younger than you. If you do not have permission to address them by the first name, then don't, even if the candidate is younger than you. Are you 50 and the candidate is 30? You still need to ask permission, like with any other adult. Are you general manager and you are interviewing (no matter why) a mechanic? Be polite. Age, profession or hierarchy do not give you the right to behave impolitely.

Be punctual. Do not leave the candidates waiting because they need a job and you are in the position to choose. To mirror what I wrote for the candidates, if you are looking for a high-level profile, you wouldn't want to offend them by showing how busy <u>you</u> are and how unimportant they are. In other words, sensible people will not accept such a behaviour, or, best case scenario, you will receive compliance but not loyalty.

Offer a minimum level of comfort: a glass of water, a normal room temperature, reduced noise level, proper lighting etc. Maybe they are minor issues to you, but they make up the big picture. Think about an interview during the summer. The candidate arrives around 3 PM, in the peak of the heat and you invite him/her to a room without air conditioning, you keep him there for at least 60 minutes, and while sweat conquers all, you are not even offering a glass of water. If you care about what the candidate will think of this company where he/she has the „great opportunity" to work, you will treat him/her better than that.

Turn off <u>your</u> telephone during the interview, or leave them in another room. If you do not positively appreciate a candidate who's telephone is ringing during the interview, I can assure you, the feeling is mutual. If you face an absolute emergency and you must receive a phone call during this particular interview, I strongly recommend to mention this in the beginning. Simply saying „I am kindly asking your understanding – I may have to answer the telephone during our conversation; I realize this is unusual, but it is also a real emergency and I apologies" will show that you have manners and also you respect the candidate enough to inform that you must take the call.

Avoid interruptions. There are few more unpleasant moments like being in the middle of a conversation when the door opens and someone calls you out of the room „for just on second", or they ask you to sign something, or whatever. Of course! Even more unpleasant is to be „urgently called by your supervisor", you leave and possibly not even return. Very likely you will also meet candidates which are not „scared" by such incidents, but also very likely you (and your boss) are being properly „labelled". If you aim for a different type of interaction, then you must prevent such events from happening.

3. Prepare for the interview

You may be working for many years for this company, you may be an experienced recruiter, but each candidate is unique. Each interview will bring you face-to-face with a unique person, different from any other persons you have met so far. And this unique person sees and understands the world through his/her unique angle. Maybe the perception of the recruiting ad is different, of course they have their own expectations of you, of your company, of their future employer, of this interview etc. For these reasons it is absolutely necessary that you prepare for it.

During the screening process you read „diagonally" this candidate's Resume, but before the interview you must pay proper attention and read carefully. Underline, highlight, write comments, transform it into the working tool it really is. Use the 3

– 4 pages you have, for the exact purpose they were sent to you!

Search this CV for relevant items for this job, and include them in your planned questions list. (Yes, the list of questions is mandatory for those of us who are not geniuses yet). This will give you the opportunity to confirm them and to obtain even more details meant to help you with the selection decision.

If you are at the short-list already, then you may try to gather references about the candidate. Networking plays an important part but even a simple internet search can return surprising and useful information.

Make sure you have a room available for the interview.

Make sure there are no overlaps in your calendar, for the duration of the interview.

Make sure you can fulfil the requirements of the section 2 above.

Make sure you have provided the candidate with all needed information to arrive easily and in time for the interview.

Make sure you have at least a basic notion about the field of activity of the recruiting field, or, if you don't, then get studying material. Imagine you are recruiting an IT Helpdesk and you cannot tell the difference between servers, work stations and peripherals. Or imagine you are recruiting an accountant and you cannot tell the difference between VAT closing and the booking of an invoice.

I remember I had to recruit and select a programmer. I remember carefully going through the profile, searching for candidates and realising that there was no 100% match (surprise, surprise!). How could I tell the difference between a shallow and a valuable candidate in a field I do not know? I couldn't do it alone. I then talked to the hiring manager and asked him to give some orientation points and a set of technical questions to apply to all candidates. I found out afterwards that my approach was appreciated by the candidates, so you can try it.

Make sure you have a „plan B", in case the candidate's answer to one of your questions is irrelevant or avoided.

Doing all of this will ensure you appear professional to the candidates and will increase your interview's efficiency, because it helps you focus on the important aspects of the selection process, without useless distractions.

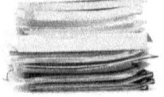

4. Avoid clichés

You may have read a number of books and articles which show you „10 questions" which guarantee your success in an interview. At that time you have assimilated them and applied them for a while, most probably until you met the 5th candidate who gave you the same answer. Yes, you guessed right: the „10 answers" who get you the job are also available.

And now that everyone knows your secret, what is to be done? As a starting point, formulate your own questions, fit for your the specific situation, rather than copying them from a book.

As a second step, avoid clichés, or, if you must use them, do this with a bit of humour, and not as if they are the absolute truth that only you hold.

Let's imagine you start an interview for a position as receptionist in a multinational company and that all steps until now, are followed. The candidate across the table has the relevant experience, meets most of the criteria and shows interest for this position. Generally, 45 – 60 minutes are allocated to an interview and if you think the candidate may also have questions, the time is usually short.

The first mistake would be to waist the first 10 minutes talking about weather. Yes, but some books advise you to „break the ice" this way ….. but what if you break the ice with something like „thank you for coming and I hope my directions were useful and you found easily our location"? If the answer comes „actually I got lost around....." then maybe you have a chance to revisit the directions you give to the candidates (useful ice breaker).

In this particular case, an useless question is „where do you see yourself in 5 years?". By far more appropriate is „are you willing to work on this position for at least 18 months?"- this is actually what you need to know, right?

A very popular question is „what salary do you want?". I personally answered this question by „15000 €". The lady in front of me looked extremely surprised and then I said „you asked me what I want, not what I would accept in order to work here". I was not selected for that job of course, but at the end of the interview I didn't want it anymore anyways. So pay attention to the phrasing of your questions; it is better to write them down and give yourself the chance to review and adjust them.

Each interview I took as a candidate between 2003 – 2006 I was amused being asked to present 3 flaws or 3 weak points about myself. To each of them I answered that I came there to get the job, and I would prefer to discuss the strengths I possess, which would get me the job. I know it is somewhat a standard question, but it would return many standard answers like „my biggest flaw is that I am an incurable perfectionist". The candidates will not deliver to you their real flaws and most of the times you will receive a bouncing answer which will not provide any truly useful information. Therefore I suggest you find some other questions who may lead you to discover what you would consider a flaw.

The last cliché example I use, largely adopted, is the problematic supervisor. This question takes various shapes, from „please tell me about one of your supervisors which you consider very difficult to deal with", to more subtle approaches like „tell us about a conflictual situation you had with one of your supervisors and how was this resolved".

I totally understand the intention of the recruiter to see whether the candidate and the future supervisor can work together, but would you really accept an employee who would denigrate any of their supervisors?! This will also be the answer you will receive in 90% of the cases, or from experienced and tactful candidates. They will tell you „conflict is a much stronger word", or „of course we had different opinions on some occasions but....", or „I have never had any conflict with either of my supervisors". And this answer is not telling anything from what you want to find out. I suggest you use a part of a situational interview or an assessment center, to discover potential compatibility issues between the candidate and the future supervisor.

5. Be honest

With a very strong wish to attract candidates (and future employees) showing the greatest performance and education, many employers over-estimate the specifics of the position, or the company situation, which create post-hiring frustrations to many of the candidates. Previously, the candidates were advised to ask clarifying questions, but a proactive attitude from your side as employer, would be very beneficial to the process.

The most common error in this category is „inflating" the characteristics of the position. We see many secretarial jobs or „computer operator" jobs, with high education as mandatory, when in fact, looking at the tasks, the high-school education would be sufficient. We see „invoicing" jobs called „computer operator" or jobs of „clerk" occupied by people with higher education. On the long run, such inconsistencies raise frustrations and unrealistic expectations.

It is a valid point that until recently, having a „better official title" would give people more opportunities to be considered for better positions and so, many employers have given this chance to their staff. I have met one woman who was working as a maid, but her employment contract stated „programmer" because she had such a qualification and she needed proof of „relevant experience". My approach to HR is to keep a very realistic picture of the positions within the company, with consistency between the tasks and the title of the positions, because this will increase the chances to attract **and keep** the right candidates.

Another frequent over-statement is the performance appraisal system. There are very few companies who actually have such a system but all of them talk about it with their candidates. Imagine you are the candidate and you find out from your future employer that „they encourage performance and want to maintain a positive internal equity especially towards loyal and efficient employees". You would probably leave thinking optimistically to your targets and how you will be rewarded for your performance. Once hired, you realise that the only existant reward for performance is that maybe your supervisor will suggest a salary increase at some point. But think about it: they did not lie to you – no performance appraisal system was mentioned, no bonus system – one can actually say that they were very honest. But could they have pictured the situation in a more realistic manner? Coming back to you as employer: what would the candidate understand if you told him/her that „our company encourages performance and wishes to maintain an internal positive equity towards loyal and efficient employees and to achieve this, we have full trust in our managers, especially that so far a complete performance appraisal system has not been implemented, because we are a rather small company. At the beginning of each fiscal year, our managers meet and decide who will receive a salary increase, as a reward for last year's performance". Now please compare the 2 phrases and notice the difference in content and message.

Lastly in this chapter, „promotion opportunities". As all the candidates have learnt that they must be ambitious and must wish promotion if they want to be considered for the hot positions, in the mirror, all employers have learnt to advertise marvellous development and promotion opportunities in their companies. The point is that of course, they are not unlimited and of course, not all employees will climb up the hierarchy ladder. Even multinational companies find it difficult to ensure equal chances to all ambitious employees, and the situation becomes even more complicated when we speak about smaller companies. Why would you create unrealistic career expectations and open the gate to frustration for your candidates? The best approach is to present the real situation and to assure them that when they are prepared for the next career step, you will support them and if this happens outside of your company, you will wish them good luck and hope that somewhere in the future you will meet again. Yes, this is exactly what I meant. Valuable people, who grow, will in fact grow more than what the company has to offer. Why limit them, out of pure selfishness? An overqualified employee will anyway get bored and leave the company.

In all my career I have personally applied this principle and had only to gain from it, especially when former employees have returned to the company on a superior position, being ready. Sincerity will grow your notoriety and will have a major positive impact on your existing and future employees. The recruiting ad is a very good place to start.

6. Use the discussion time efficiently

We briefly touched this in the section about respect, but this is a very important aspect, so we will treat it separately.

Often, the interview is seen as a game; a series of trap questions who will reveal the „true colours" of the candidate – something he/she would not have wanted us to know, but we were clever enough and find it out by ourselves. In the heat of the game, some interviewers get lost in their own questions; and if they meet a candidate who understands the game and fights back (but throwing them off pace for example), then they are totally lost.

Such an interview, can be useful if conducted properly. But be sure you can make it through, before you start, otherwise, after the usual 45 – 60 minutes, you will realise you found out more about yourself, rather than the candidate. Extensive practice is needed for anyone to master this technique. Otherwise, it's like an young driver testing a Ferrari. The driver may think they did a test, but it doesn't mean they „revealed" important aspects compared to the full potential of the car.

Another frequent error is the personal curiosity of the interviewer. Something in the candidate's CV has caught your attention and even if it is not connected to the vacancy, you are losing time asking questions about it. You are creating at least 2 disadvantages:

a. you will not have enough time left for relevant questions

b. some candidates may find it intrusive and may respond directly: „how is this related to the job?"

It is also true that the candidates should include in their CV only relevant information and then you may also react „honestly, I don't know, but if you wrote it there I thought it must be a connection". And now, like the joke says, you are both right, but it doesn't matter anyway. It would be much more useful to keep the conversation to the point.

Remind yourself all the time what was the purpose of the interview. What exactly do you want to know from the candidate? Efficiency means achieving your goals in due time. Some of my colleagues used to write this on the interview chart and said that seeing it in front of their eyes helped them stay on track. It is important to keep the objective clear in your mind.

In this context, we recall candidates who talk too much. A candidate who is asked about his thesis for the Berlin University will end up telling you about the coffee bar in the German Television tower. And, he/she talks so casually and uses good humour that you forget your initial question. It is your role to lead this conversation and to help the candidates answer the questions as concise as possible, or you will not have the chance to ask too many questions in this meeting. It is also in the interest of the candidate that you find out your relevant information by the end of the interview. So make sure the discussion remains in the desired frame.

7. Be aware of the company culture

In any given moment of your professional life, you must be aware of the environment you're working in, but especially if we think about „the right person in the right place" as a motto of any HR department. When our task is to bring together individuals who will work as a team, this becomes essential. It may seem strange to talk about it here, when in theory it starts from the job design, but in most cases, the job specification allows for interpretation and in those areas where you can „slide", it is best to remember the exact culture for which you are recruiting.

If you are recruiting for a bank, a culture strongly lead by regulations and procedures, it will be strange to look for an entrepreneurial personality.

But if you are recruiting for a start-up marketing agency, then you may wish to avoid candidates who only feel safe working with strict rules.

It is very useful to make the link with the department climate and the manager's personality, when you are recruiting. It will not be enough to hire the best candidate, if they drive anyone crazy in the first 2 months and also cumulate frustration because they do not fit in. The effect may not be totally negative, but the performance of the team will suffer for sure and very likely the new employee will take the next train out. If your former candidate – the new frustrated employee - concludes that you have intentionally mislead him/her, your professional image will suffer.

Maybe you did not intend for it, but for sure you provided vague or incomplete information and now it's even irrelevant why it happened, but only that it happened. Very important aspect, especially with the increased pressure on selection.

We all know from our marketing classes that „advertising is the soul of business" and that „the package is the product" and we have seen the same reality being described in more or less attractive manners. The HR department's performance started to be measured against the duration of the recruiting process and in this context, the urge to paint the company picture as warm as possible appears logical. But we must refrain from omitting details or from „warming the picture" too much because we harm ourselves on the long run. Strongly related to Section 5 of this chapter, about honesty, ignorance also does not come cheap.

On a short term, you could tick a fast hire. Congratulations! On the medium term, a person, let's say too different in a culture averse to diversity will lead to a departing employee and then you start again. I advise everyone to choose carefully; we do not fit everywhere, in any particular moment of our life and career, and the best approach is to move towards places who encourage our development and not our retrogression.

We shouldn't reinvent ourselves for each new job; we mustn't „brainwash" the new employees – it is much better to choose the ones with positive integration predictability.

8. Avoid monologues

We reached a subject creating anger and frustration. Unfortunately only those recruiters who remember what it's like to be a candidate, remember this.

As mentioned already, the time is never enough for the interview. There are many things to find out about the candidate and it is sometimes very difficult to reveal important traits, especially if the candidate conceils them for the moment. Then why, as interviewer, would we start monologues? Why would we waste time to express a personal opinion about one or the other topic?

I am sure there are multiple possible answers to this question and some even have a point, but let's remember again why are we meeting the candidate. We did not call them out of personal curiosity. Even more, most of the candidates will be annoyed.

A valid endeavour is to test the candidate and give the illusion of a personal opinion, even different from one minute to the next, to see if our candidate stands his/her ground or not, or to see him/her avoiding (or not) a mini-conflict.

But this is totally different than talking for minutes about your personal interests. The purpose of the interview is to bring valuable information into the selection process. What information can you obtain by having your monologue? During the interview you must play a well-defined role, with a well-defined purpose to obtain a very realistic opinion about the candidate in front of you.

I remember a gentlemen with a very important position, who had been a candidate recently and said about my colleague: „I was not very impressed by Mrs. X during the interview". „Why?" I asked. „She was asking stupid questions about basic knowledge and after a while she forgot what I told her". The lady he talked about knew very well what she was doing. Her questions aimed at the candidate's knowledge and her „amnesia" pointed exactly at his reaction. Surprisingly, he didn't realise it even retrospectively and he thought that he has enough data to assess the interviewer, without considering the role she was playing. This is an accurate indication about the candidate's professional maturity. Important take-out from this section is that during the interview we have to obtain information, so, as the proverb advises: „we have 2 ears and only one mouth, for us to hear more and talk less".

9. Take notes

Frantically write down everything the candidate tells you. From troubles with their children to the tasks they had in their projects, from the structure of the department to the manager's personality, everything could become helpful at some point.

During the interview, you could assess competencies. If you only write down the result, you could forget what triggered the conclusion and if you meet 2 candidates with equal results, you will not have enough arguments in either's favour.

In short: write as much as possible. It will help you later, after you have seen 10 candidates, some of them with similar experiences, and for sure you go back to the CVs and try to remember detail. When criteria seem to produce equal scores and when we need more details, without the notes, your memory will be put to a difficult test.

But if you have detailed notes, you will easily remember the discussions, the nuances, the subtle messages, and it will be easier to obtain a ranking.

10. Smile

I saved the best for last.

The smile has been used for ever with various meanings in many of the terrestrial cultures, at least. Seventeen muscles contribute to this exclusively human trait, which speaks about good mood and which stimulates the production of endorphins in the brain, the „happiness hormone". In other words, a discrete smile will project a friendlier person and will help you feel better.

Imagine you are a candidate and that the interviewer speaks with some sort of grimace and with a frown. Everything says tension, pressure, dissatisfaction. Will you ask yourself if maybe you are the reason for this acute discomfort? Will you ask yourself if this is the general mood in that company? Will you have doubts about this potential employer?

If your answer is „yes" at any of these questions, then be sure your interlocutors will feel the same.

But if you smiled a little, not too much, not faking, but just a little, just to send the message that you are happy to meet them; just to create a friendly atmosphere during the interview; just to make sure that the candidate's attention is on the topics discussed and not on your reasons to be upset.... How would that be? Would the candidate relax a bit? Will the candidate say they are glad to meet you? Will they answer more openly and will give you more information? Will this contribute a bit to their wish to join your team?

The candidate is never an adversary, but a discussion partner. You are not supposed to „catch them off guard" or to corner them, but only to understand them. Give them a smile; give yourself a smile in the mirror before each meeting, and then note the effects.